THE ROBIN MAKES A LAUGHING SOUND

a birder's observations

Sallie Wolf

DESIGNED BY
MICAH BORNSTEIN

imagine!

*To Hilde and Lou Wolf, with love,
and in memory of John Trott—S. W.*

With help from Rachel and Beckett—M. B.

At the time of publication, any URLs printed in this book were accurate and
active. Charlesbridge and the author are not responsible for the content or
accessibility of any URL that may have changed.

An Imagine Book
Published by Charlesbridge
85 Main Street
Watertown, MA 02472
(617) 926-0329
www.imaginebooks.net

Library of Congress Cataloging-in-Publication Data Available
ISBN 978-1-58089-318-3 (reinforced for library use)
ISBN 978-1-60734-190-1 (ebook pdf)

Printed in China
(hc) 10 9 8 7 6 5 4 3 2

Illustrations done in watercolor and pen and ink on Sallie's
    original journal pages and on handmade paper,
    then scanned and manipulated in Photoshop
Display type and text type set in Muriel and Rochelle,
    designed by Ellinor Maria Rapp, and Sabon
Color separations by Chroma Graphics, Singapore
Printed by 1010 Printing International Limited in
    Huizhou, Guangdong, China
Production supervision by Brian G. Walker
Designed by Micah Bornstein

CONTENTS

AUTHOR'S NOTE

Hawk

Canada
goose

My seventh-grade teacher taught our class to identify birds using Roger Tory Peterson's *A Field Guide to the Birds of Eastern and Central North America*. We set up bird feeders on the flat roof outside our classroom. The birds became used to feeding there, and we soon learned to identify the different species. Then we set out metal cage traps and began to operate a bird-banding station. We kept detailed records about the birds we caught and sent copies of our records to the US Fish and Wildlife Service.

We also studied bird behavior. One time I brought a stuffed owl to class, and we set it on the rooftop. Not a single bird would come to our feeders while the owl was on the roof. A flock of blue jays gathered in the trees nearby, calling and scolding. My teacher warned me that the jays might dive-bomb my owl and damage it. Was I willing to take that risk for the opportunity to observe bird behavior? I was. We watched for an hour or more, taking notes. Our homework that night was to write up our observations.

I have been bird-watching ever since.

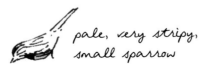

pale, very stripy, small sparrow

6

goldfinch

BIRD-WATCHING

Robins come in springtime.
In summer they nest here.
Warblers are just passing through.
Cardinals stay all year.

Juncos come in winter,
thrushes in the fall.
Some birds never come here.
I don't see them at all.

robin

In the spring & in the fall—
warblers passing through

common yellowthroat

SPRING

goldfinch
robin
fox sparrow
Canada goose
brown creeper
scarlet tanager
house sparrow
red-breasted nuthatch
catbird
cardinal   pigeon
great blue heron
junco
hermit thrush
starling
downy woodpecker
mourning dove
chipping sparrow
white-throated sparrow
mystery sparrow
blue jay
crow   grackle
chickadee
gull

crocus

white oak

WARBLERS:
yellow-rumped
Nashville
ovenbird
black-throated green
magnolia
palm
Tennessee
Cape May
black-and-white
yellow
chestnut-sided
common yellowthroat
redstart

Early crocuses
burst through dead leaves. Brown creepers
circle up tree trunks.

brown creeper

March 26—I saw a cardinal
& a robin perched in the same
young maple, both singing.

THE ROBIN MAKES A LAUGHING SOUND

The robin makes a laughing sound.
It makes me stop and look around
to see just what the robin sees—
fresh new leaves on twigs of trees,
a strong, high branch on which to rest,
a safe, dry ledge to hold its nest.
The robin makes a laughing sound.
I stop. I always look around.

The robin makes a laughing sound
Reminding me to look around
~~At buds on twig tips swelling big~~
~~And swelling worms which~~
~~robins dig~~

Look up! Look up!
Geese are calling.
Look up! Look up!
Gulls are laughing.

scarlet tanager

April 23—First sighting of a
white throat—I've been hearing
them for about 3 days.

white-throated
sparrow

bloodroot

BIRDS I
KNOW ARE
NESTING
HERE:
robin
cardinal
chickadee
blue jay
mourning dove
kestrel
pigeon
starling
house sparrow
crow
downy woodpecker
goldfinch

baby house sparrows,
flopping around
on the sidewalk

April 28—Robin with a beak
full of nesting material,
perched on a twig & calling
its laughing call. Oh—
which way did it go?

RIDDLE

Not
a circle,
but round.
Blue, white, or
green—some are
s p e c k l e d
b r o w n.

Once
they are
Peck-peck-

Peckled, I find
two pieces on
the ground.

HAPPY ENDING?

This April morning I watched
one red-breasted nuthatch work its way
headfirst down the trunk of my maple tree. A tiny bird—
short stubby tail, striped eye—it bobbed its beak,
searching the bark for food.

A pair of nuthatches used to visit my feeder every day.
That was before West Nile virus
spread from bird to bird.
It decimated the crows and other birds as well.

The news said chickadees were hit hard. I couldn't tell—
they still fed in my yard.
But I've waited three years
to see red-breasted nuthatches feeding here.

May 2—The black cap sits on its head like a black beret.

catbird

May 8—Catbirds in the pagoda dogwood. They seem very shy and secretive. One year there were babies—fledglings—in August. Do they nest in my yard?

grackle

May 15—The male cardinal put a seed (I think) in the bill of the female cardinal.

pansies

15

SUMMER

blue jay
goldfinch
kestrel
cardinal
crow
house sparrow
mourning dove
flicker
starling
pigeon
gull
chickadee
chimney swift
grackle
robin

white oak—leaves look
like weird footprints

Wobbly starling babes—
striped beggars pleading for food.
Feed me, feed me first!

17

August 29—A young robin tried to land on a single wire, but couldn't catch its balance. Kept fluttering its wings, using its tail, turned around, abandoned ship, & flew into the lilacs.

rose

goldfinch

18

SEAGULLS

Seagulls hang out at the mall.
They laugh. They squawk. They strut.
They're not shy.
They travel in packs,
fighting over french fries
and scraps of burgers—
just like the kids from middle school,
who hang out at the mall.

FRUSTRATION

I often hear what I can't see—
birds and squirrels scolding me.
I scan the branches far and near,
but I don't see what I can hear.

dove

The loon is a bird of northern lakes.

The chipping sparrow is the smallest
  sparrow I know,
with a rust-brown cap & a black line
  across its brow.
It pecks on the edges of the road
  and flies away when I get too close.
Its song sounds like the whir of a
  sewing machine, but musical.
Maybe this year it will nest here.

chipping sparrow

Hear that eerie laughing call he makes?

ROBINS TAKE A BATH

Flippy-floppy, splishy-sploshy—
robins take a bath.
One bird, two birds, three birds, four—
it's crowded. Splishy-splash!

Hip-hop squirrel comes to drink.
Robins flutter, fly.
Down jumps squirrel. Birds return
from where they perched nearby.

Fluffy fledglings preen their feathers.
Four birds fly away.
Freshly groomed and tidy robins,
finished for the day.

September 6—Hawk in my maple tree—
no wonder things seemed quiet.
Whatever made me look up?

mystery sparrow

Flippy-floppy-splash

~~When the~~ Hip-hop squirrel comes
to drink
Robins flutter-fly.
Down hops jumps squirrel.
~~Robins~~ Birds return
~~Back into the bath~~
sky—high—bye—nearby—

squirrel

FALL

Cooper's hawk
mourning dove
pigeon
Canada goose
white-breasted nuthatch
flicker
cardinal
wild turkey
robin
white-throated sparrow
junco
starling
chickadee
winter wren
house sparrow
white-crowned sparrow
cedar waxwing
crow
great horned owl
brown creeper
hermit thrush
blue jay

Cooper's hawk

geese

Bare branches scrape sky.
Cooper's hawk strikes silently.
Pigeons, doves—beware!

mourning dove

WHITE-BREASTED NUTHATCH

The white-breasted nuthatch is fond of suet.
She hangs upside down from the feeder and pecks.
There's nothing to it!

a flicker, eating ants

wild turkey

September 28—I saw lots of robins this morning, massing to migrate, I guess. There's a white-throated sparrow in my yard; juncos are back.
There was a red-breasted nuthatch on my maple. I can hear chickadees now.

robin

WINTER WREN

Are you a winter wren?
I see you only once or twice a year—
a tiny, dark shadow scooting under bushes.
If your tail weren't so perky,
if you weren't so tiny,
I'd think you were one of those
ubiquitous sparrows.

winter wren

cedar waxwing

October 5—Who makes that sound? I haven't heard that one before.

crow

Who is he scolding?

December 6—This morning
I heard a loud crow
commotion. I looked up to see
crows flocking to one tree.
They seemed to be circling
in to one place so I looked,
not really expecting to see
anything, but there was an
owl. Big, brown, w/ feather
horns, a reddish tail.
I counted over 50 crows.
They flew around &
threatened. Finally the
owl took off & all the crows
with it.

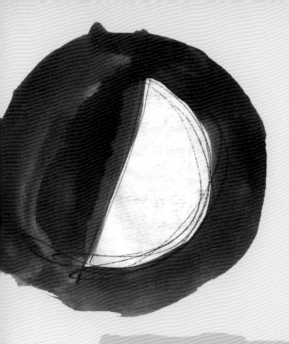

GREAT HORNED OWL

An owl once perched in my tree
at night (when most birds cannot see).
But when the sun rose,
he was found by some crows,
and their caws caused the owl to flee.

Do owls migrate?

31

WINTER

tufted titmouse
chickadee
junco
cardinal

downy woodpecker
crow

red-breasted nuthatch

blue jay
pigeon
starling

house sparrow

mourning dove

tufted titmouse

Some white oaks keep their leaves all winter.

Like the melting snow,
January slips away.
Hear the chickadee?

33

JUNCOS

Snow flurries off and on,
but nothing stays
this bitter-cold, gray January day.
A flock of juncos
feeds among the weeds,
scratching the dirt
in search of hidden seeds.

Two juncos fly at each other,
tails flashing white,
batting wings—courtship or fight?
Snowflakes fill the air.
The juncos stay,
two smoldering dark coals
this gray January day.

February 3—The cardinal just munches until the seed in its beak opens and the shells drop away. What bird is it that flicks seeds left & right out of the feeder until it finds just the one it wants?

CARDINALS

Rubies in the snow,
berry beaks.
Twelve cardinals in my snowy backyard.
Six pairs!

You are friends now, companions.
But when the snow melts,
when your colors fade a little,
when it's nesting time?

I remember two red enemies last spring,
chasing, chasing each other through
  my obstacle-course backyard.
Over the fence. Under the maple.
  Around the house. Into the alley.
A two-week-long tournament to win this territory.

But when the nesting is done, the babies grown,
when leaves turn the colors of cardinals?
You are friends again,
companions for the lonely winter.

February 19—Where do birds
sleep at night?

A cardinal
swooped right
past me.

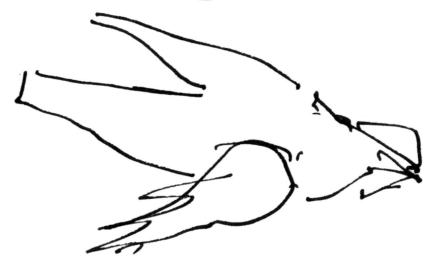

Drilling holes rat-a-
tat-tat
Checkerboard upon
his back
Black & white
Swooping flight

Square of red ~~on the~~
back of his head

downy woodpecker
swinging around
tree, like a waltz

flicker

DOWNY WOODPECKER

Checkerboard back,
white and black.
Patch of red
upon his head.
King me!

39

March 2—The blue jay mimics a chickadee.

JUNCOS AND ROBINS

Juncos in October,
robins in the spring.
Birds chatter in the winter.
In March they start to sing.

When juncos leave for farther north,
robins come to nest.
Junco? Robin? I can't tell
which one I like the best.

One speaks to me of gray and white,
of winter winds and snow.
One returns to feed on worms
when warmer breezes blow.

Juncos every winter,
robins every spring.
Juncos chatter in the snow.
In March the robins sing.

ABOUT MY JOURNALS

I have been writing journals and diaries since seventh grade, inspired in part by my favorite novel, *Two Little Savages* by Ernest Thompson Seton. The novel's main character, Yan, studies plants, birds, and other animals by sketching in a notebook.

Over time I have adapted my style of journal keeping to suit my needs. First I ignored the dates at the tops of the pages; then I began to buy blank books. As drawing became more important to me, I switched from lined journals to unlined sketchbooks. I decided to begin each entry with the date, the place, the time, and the weather. That way my pen is already moving before I have to think about what to write. In addition, I keep a list of the birds I see each day.

While I have always included notes about birds in my journals, I also write about my feelings, what I yearn for, who I like, what I want to do with my life. I write about what I'm thinking, books I'm reading, ideas that intrigue me, and projects I want to work on. I write about everything and anything that pops into my head.

Some of my journals are leather-bound books with beautiful paper. Some of my journals I bind myself. Many of my journals I buy at the art supply store. I write with a real fountain pen and travel with a bottle of ink and a set of watercolor paints. I am almost never without my journal. It is where all my art and writing begins.

RESOURCES

All About Birds
https://www.allaboutbirds.org
Sponsored by the Cornell Lab of Ornithology, one of the premier research centers for bird study. Includes a guide to the birds of North America, tips for attracting birds to your yard, ways to become involved in bird conservation, and interactive links where you can participate in several research studies. Also features special pages for teachers.

Arnold, Caroline. *Birds: Nature's Magnificent Flying Machines.* Watertown, MA: Charlesbridge, 2003.

Audubon
www.audubon.org/birds
Links to an online field guide as well as information about birds in need of conservation efforts and reproductions of Audubon's engravings of American birds.

Bird Watching in the USA and Around the World
http://www.birding.com/
Includes links and fact sheets for hundreds of different bird species from around the world as well as videos, tips for bird identification, and a list of top bird websites.

Collard, Sneed B., III. *Beaks!* Watertown, MA: Charlesbridge, 2002.

Peterson, Roger Tory. *A Field Guide to the Birds of Eastern and Central North America.* 5th ed. Boston: Houghton Mifflin, 2002.

Seton, Ernest Thompson. *Two Little Savages: Being the Adventures of Two Boys Who Lived as Indians and What They Learned.* New York: Dover Publications, 1962.

Sibley, David Allen. *The Sibley Guide to Birds*, Second Edition. New York: Alfred A. Knopf, 2014. In addition to this guide to all North American birds, there are specialized editions for birds in the eastern and western parts of the continent as well as guides to bird behavior.

Weindensaul, Scott. *Birds.* National Audubon Society First Field Guides. New York: Scholastic, 1998.